HEATHCLIFF ROUND 3

The funniest feline in America delights millions of fans every day as he appears in over 500 newspapers. You'll have a laugh a minute as Heathcliff tangles with the milkman, the fish store owner, the tuna fisherman and just about everyone else he runs into. If you're looking for some fun, look no further, Heathcliff is here.

Heathcliff Books

HEATHCLIFF

ROUND 3

by

Geo Gately

CHARTER BOOKS, NEW YORK

HEATHCLIFF ROUND 3

A Charter Book / published by arrangement with
McNaught Syndicate, Inc.

PRINTING HISTORY
Charter Original / February 1984
Third printing / September 1984

ISBN: 0-441-32228-X

Charter Books are published by The Berkley Publishing Group,
200 Madison Avenue, New York, New York 10016.
PRINTED IN THE UNITED STATES OF AMERICA

"HEATHCLIFF!...HAVE YOU NO CONSCIENCE?!"

"AH!... THE TAROT CARDS NEVER LIE!"

"IT'S HEATHCLIFF'S OLD NEIGHBORHOOD!"

"SOMETHING FOR A SHUT-IN."

"GET IN HERE WITH MY SHAVING CREAM!"

"AW, C'MON!...SELL ME THE NEGATIVE!"

"MAKE UP YOUR MIND!... IT'S EITHER ME
OR THE MASCOT!"

"STOP PLAYING WITH YOUR FOOD!"

"HE CAN ALWAYS PICK OUT THE VETERINARIAN!"

"ZAP!...RIGHT IN FRONT OF THE ASSEMBLY!
...A HERRING SHOOTS OUT OF MY TROMBONE!"

"I HATE THESE HALFTIME CEREMONIES!"

"WELL!...I SEE WE'RE ALL HOME FROM A HARD DAY!"

"HE HATES TO DUMP AN EMPTY CAN!"

"I'LL SEE THAT MOTHER GETS THEM!"

"GETTING PRETTY TRICKY, AREN'T WE ?!"

"I NABBED HEATHCLIFF RED HANDED, SARGE!...
...HE WON'T SLIP AWAY THIS TIME!"

"WE SAW THAT DOLLAR FIRST!"

"WE'LL FLIP YA FOR IT."

"HE CERTAINLY TAKES GOOD CARE
OF HIS FAVORITE TREE."

"OKAY!...SO I FUMBLED THE KICKOFF!!"

"I'M SORRY ABOUT LAST YEAR!"

"GRANDMA, SOMEONE PUT BUBBLEGUM
IN MY TROMBONE!"

"GET OFF THE CAT WALK!"

" TENDER SNAILS AND LOBSTER TAILS...

...THAT'S WHAT LITTLE CATS ARE MADE OF!"

"I'M TELLING YOU!...IT
WAS A FLYING SAUCER!"

"I'LL KNOW WHEN MY COFFEE BREAK IS OVER!"

"YOU DIDN'T *HAVE* TO COME!"

"HE WON'T BE BACK 'TILL NEXT YEAR."

"THIS IS AN AQUARIUM!"

"THE TAX COLLECTOR TAKES A BIG BITE!"

"BON VOYAGE!"

"SCRAM, NEIGHBOR!"

"WHAT A CHEAP DOG WHISTLE!.... I DIDN'T
HEAR ANYTHING, DID YOU?"

9-18 © 1980
McNaught Synd., Inc.

"THAT WAS A COTTON SWAB...
...NOW FOR THE SHOT..."

"YOU SAVED THE CATCH!"

"HEATHCLIFF, WILL YOU PLEASE STOP MIXING UP
THOSE HOT TODDIES?!"

"NOW I KNOW HOW A POT ROAST FEELS!"

"YOU'RE GIVING THE SAFETY PATROL A BAD NAME!"

"WERE YOU DIGGING UP THAT GARDEN AGAIN ?!"

"THE MEAT TENDERIZER?...HEATHCLIFF HAS IT."

"OBJECTION!...THE PROSECUTION IS BAITING THE WITNESS!"

" HIS TUNNEL CAVED IN. "

"CRAZY SHIRLEY?"

"I BAGGED EIGHT TROUT!...THERE MIGHT
EVEN BE ONE IN HERE FOR HEATHCLIFF!"

" HE PREFERS TO WAIT FOR GIGI. "

"THERE YOU ARE, GENTLEMEN!....ONE MORE REASON
FOR AN INCREASED DEFENSE BUDGET!"

"IT'S HIS BIRTHDAY, SO I GIFTWRAPPED ONE!"

"YOU'LL EAT WHEN I'M READY!"

"HAH!... CAUGHT YOU RED-HANDED!"

"ANNOYING THE REF WON'T HELP!"

"WATCH OUT...HE'S LOADING UP THE SNOWBALLS!"

"ANY REQUESTS?"

"..YOUR CONTRIBUTION TO
THIS WORTHY CANDIDATE
WILL BE GREATLY....

... SHREDDER,
PLEASE."

© 1980
McNaught Synd., Inc.

10-1

"I THOUGHT I TOOK YOU OFF
BETWEEN MEAL SNACKS?!"

"YOU DIDN'T WASH YOUR NECK!"

"JUST AS I SUSPECTED...SCRATCHING POST ELBOW."

"CALL THE OFFICE, DEAR AND TELL THEM
I'LL BE LATE."

"OH-OH!...GRANDMA WILL *LOVE* THIS!...
COO-COO STEW!"

"CHRISTMAS IS OVER!...THEY JUST FORGOT TO TAKE THE SIGN DOWN!"

"GRAN'MA!"

" HICCUPS. "

"IT'S A TRICK, YOUR HONOR!... THE WITNESS IS PERFECTLY SANE!"

"JUST BECAUSE YOU'RE A GENIUS, GRANDPA, DOESN'T MEAN I'LL BE ONE."

"THE ANNUAL HEATHCLIFF 'BALONEY' AWARD!"

"ISN'T THAT SWEET ?!...HE'S WARMING UP OUR BATH WATER!"

WE NETTED TWO TONS OF TUNA...

...AND THIRTEEN POUNDS OF STOWAWAY.

"HE NEVER MISSES THE GOTTBUX MANSION!"

"SO MUCH FOR 'SALMON SURPRISE'!"

"HE'LL SHOW AND I'LL TELL."

"HE'S DECIDED NOT TO HAVE TURKEY THIS YEAR!"

"ACCORDING TO THIS, HE'S BEING DEPORTED!"

"DON'T CALL HIM FOR SUPPER WHEN I'M RAKING...

...LEAVES."

"...AND WHAT WOULD LITTLE ORPHAN ANNIE LIKE FOR CHRISTMAS ?!"

"HOW MANY TICKETS DID YOU GIVE OUT ?!"

"WOW!...A CLOCK FOR EACH OF US!"

"I CALL THIS 'CHEF'S SURPRISE'."

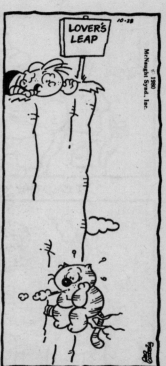

"ALL CLEAR ... CRAZY
SHIRLEY WENT HOME."

"LET ME KNOW IF HE BOTHERS YOU."

"NOT BAD, NOT BAD!"

"HE ALWAYS LETS THE NEIGHBORHOOD KNOW
WHAT HE'S HAVING FOR DINNER!"

"NO, YOU DO NOT HAVE TO VISIT SANTA CLAUS!"

"LET'S SEE THE REPORT CARD."

"I'LL CALL MY OWN PLAYS, THANK YOU!"

"I THINK YOU MADE THE PUNCH A LITTLE STRONG."

"THE YULETIDE SPIRIT MAY WARM
HIS COLD HEART!"

"I'M GLAD **SOMEBODY** IS GOING TO RING IN THE NEW YEAR!"

"SONJA HATES CRAZY SHIRLEY."

"THEY'VE OPENED A MALL!"

"CAN YOU PICK HIM OUT?"

"COO....   ...MAY DAY! MAY DAY!"

"FOR ONCE WE GOT UNDERWAY WITHOUT HEATHCLIFF!"

"DIDN'T I SAY 'NO PETS IN THE CLASSROOM'?!"

"HE KEEPS STEALING THE SCENE!"

"HAVE YOU SEEN HEATHCLIFF'S SCRATCHING POST?"

"BATTERED, BUT UNBOWED, THE VALIANT MILKMAN
VOWED TO CONTINUE HIS APPOINTED ROUNDS AND..."

"WHOO!...CHRISTMAS TREES ARE EXPENSIVE
THIS YEAR!"

"ME, COACH!... YOU, MASCOT!!"

"HE TRIES TO BRING THEM IN FOR A LANDING."

"KITTY COMPUTER FUN... ONLY $79.95!"

"HEATHCLIFF!...I RECOGNIZED YOU RIGHT AWAY!"

"IN SEARCH OF WILD TURKEY, PILGRIM?"

"THANKS FOR THE LESSON, BUT I KNOW HOW TO USE IT."

" I THINK HE'LL FIND IT ! "

"NEXT."

"NO THANKS.... I JUST CAN'T LOOK
AT ANY MORE TURKEY!"

"THAT WAS QUITE A BACK FENCE BASH LAST NIGHT!"

"UMM...ERR...MR.GAFFNEY....I'D LIKE TO
SPEAK TO YOU ABOUT A RAISE..."

"THIS NEW GUY WON'T LAST LONG!"

"THE TUNA FLEET'S IN TOWN!"

" YOU KICKED IT.... YOU CAN GO GET IT ! "

"THIS IS THE MOST RIDICULOUS FOX HUNT
I'VE EVER BEEN ON!"

"HE'S QUITE THE COMEDIAN!"

"THERE'S NO SUCH THING AS A FREE LUNCH!"